MINISTRY OF MUNITIONS.

Technical Department—Aircraft Production.

I.C. 626.

Kingsway,

W.C. 2.

Report on
Hannoveraner Biplane.

JULY, 1918.

The Naval & Military Press Ltd

Published by
The Naval & Military Press Ltd
5 Riverside, Brambleside, Bellbrook
Industrial Estate, Uckfield, East Sussex,
TN22 1QQ England

Tel: +44 (0) 1825 749494
Fax: +44 (0) 1825 765701

www.naval-military-press.com
www.military-genealogy.com

In reprinting in facsimile from the original, any imperfections are inevitably reproduced and the quality may fall short of modern type and cartographic standards.

MINISTRY OF MUNITIONS.

Technical Department—Aircraft Production.

I.C. 626.

Kingsway,

W.C. 2.

Report on
Hannoveraner Biplane.

JULY, 1918.

REPORT ON THE
HANNOVERANER BIPLANE.

This machine was brought down by anti-aircraft fire near Lestrem, on March 29th, 1918. As will be seen from the photographs, it is of highly characteristic design, and possesses numerous features of interest.

On labels protected by celluloid, and on the upper surfaces of the wings and fuselage, are identification marks with the date 15/2/18, showing that this machine is of recent construction.

Generally speaking, the construction is of wood throughout, steel being used sparingly, except in the interplane struts, landing chasis struts, centre section and some details of the tail.

Judged by contemporary British standards of design, the Hannoveraner biplane reaches a fairly high level, the construction throughout being sound, and the finish quite good.

The performance of the machine is not by any means bad.

The leading particulars of the machine are as follows:—

Weight Empty	1,732 lbs.
Total Weight	2,572 lbs.
Area of Upper Wings	217.6 sq. ft.
Area of Lower Wings	142.4 sq. ft.
Total Area of Wings	360.0 sq. ft.
Loading per sq. ft. of Wing Surface	7.29 lbs.
Area of Aileron, each	16.4 sq. ft.
Area of Balance of Aileron	1.6 sq. ft.
Area of Top Plane of Tail	10.0 sq. ft.
Area of Bottom Plane of Tail	19.2 sq. ft.
Total Area of Tail Plane	29.2 sq. ft.
Area of Fin	6.5 sq. ft. approx.
Area of Rudder	6.4 sq. ft.
Area of Elevators	22.0 sq. ft.
Horizontal Area of Body	53.2 sq. ft.
Vertical Area of Body	91.6 sq. ft.
Total Weight per H.P.	14.3 lbs. per H.P.
Crew	Pilot and Observer.
Armament	1 Spandau firing through propeller. 1 Parabellum on ring mounting.
Engine	Opel Argus, 180 H.P.
Petrol Capacity	37¼ gallons.
Oil capacity	3 gallons.

PERFORMANCE.

(a) Climb to 5,000 ft.	7 mins.
Rate of climb in ft. per min.	590.
Indicated air speed	68.
Revolutions of Engine	1,495.
(b) Climb to 10,000 ft.	18 mins.
Rate of climb in ft. per min.	340.
Indicated air speed	65.
Revolutions of Engine	1,475.
(c) Climb to 13,000 ft.	29 mins. 45 secs.
Rate of climb in ft. per min.	190.
Indicated air speed	62.
Revolutions of Engine	1,445.

SPEED.

At 10,000 ft. 96 miles an hour; Revolutions, 1,565.
At 13,000 89½ miles an hour; Revolutions, 1,520.

Service ceiling at which rate of climb is 100 ft. per min.	15,000.
Estimated absolute ceiling	16,500.
Greatest height reached	14,400 in 39 mins. 10 secs.
Rate of climb at this height	120 ft. per min.
Air endurance	About 2½ hours at full speed at 10,000 ft., including climb to this height.
Military load	545 lbs.

STABILITY.

The machine is nose-heavy with the engine off, and slightly tail-heavy with the engine on. It tends to turn to the left with the engine on.

CONTROLLABILITY.

The machine is generally light on controls, except that the elevator seems rather insufficient at slow speeds. It is not very tiring to fly, and pulls up very quickly on landing.

VIEW.

The view is particularly good for both pilot and observer. The former sits with his eyes on a level with the top plane, and also enjoys a good view below him on account of the narrow chord of the lower plane.

CONSTRUCTION.

WINGS.

The general arrangement of the Hannoveraner wings is somewhat reminiscent of the R.E.8, except, of course, that the bottom planes have no ailerons. The upper wings are practically flat in end elevation, but the lower have pronounced dihedral angles of 2.7 deg., and are set with a positive stagger of 2 ft. 7½ in. The chord of the upper plane is 5 ft. 10¾ in., and that of the lower plane 4 ft. 3 in. In flying position, therefore, the trailing edge of the lower plane is slightly in advance of that of the upper plane. The angles of incidence marked on the manufacturer's rigging diagram, which is fixed to the side of the fuselage, and stamped on the fabric of the wing, are as follows:—

    Lower Wings   ...   ...   5½ deg. at fuselage.

                                        5 deg. at struts.

    Top Wings   ...   ...   5 deg. throughout.

The lower wings are carried direct from the bottom edge of the fuselage, the roots of the upper planes being carried on a rigidly constructed centre section, which embraces the radiator and the gravity feed petrol tank. The rearward portion of the centre section is cut away immediately over the pilot's seat and at this point the wing is about 1 ft. above the upper surface of the fuselage. The lower plane has no very pronounced wash-out, but this feature is more noticeable in the upper plane, and is enhanced by the design of the ailerons, the tips of which are set at a slightly negative angle. This gives the characteristic German appearance to the aeroplane when seen in flight. In contrast with that of the majority of German aeroplanes, the wing section is rather flatter than usual Fig. 1.

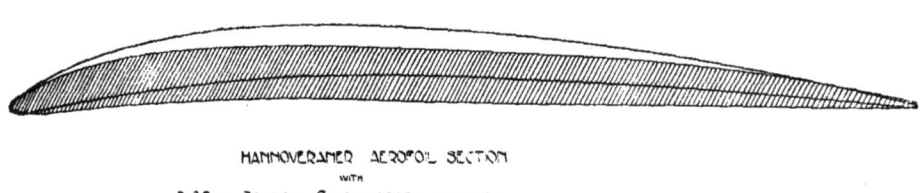

HANNOVERANER AEROFOIL SECTION
WITH
R.A.F. 14 SECTION SUPERIMPOSED —SHADED—

Fig. 1.

In Fig. 2 is given a scale drawing of the complete rib. The spars are of the usual built-up hollow section. The attachement between the wings and the fuselage is such as to permit quick detachability in case of need. It consists of a simple ball and keyhole socket device. The spars terminate in steel boxes with horizontal slots which engage with knobs or balls mounted on the fuselage members. On entering the knobs into the slots and sliding the wings backwards for a distance of ¼ in., the necks of the balls are engaged with the constricted part of the slots, and are then maintained in this position by vertical bolts passing through the spar boxes.

Spring doors are fitted on the lower plane to allow of the inspection of the pulleys for the aileron control wires.

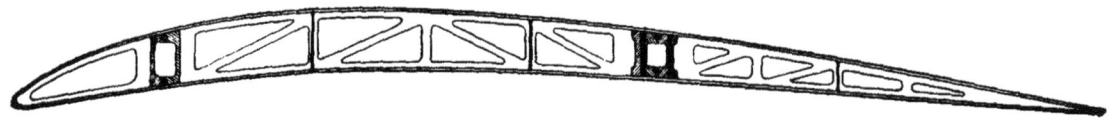

Fig. 2.

STRUTS.

These are of plain steel tubing of 1⅜ in. diameter, and are fitted with wooden fairings, secured by wrappings of fabric, the final section being of fair streamline form with a length of 4⅜ in. and a breadth of 1¾ in. The ends of the strut tubes are tapered, welded up and drilled, the method of attachment to the spars being shown in Fig. 3.

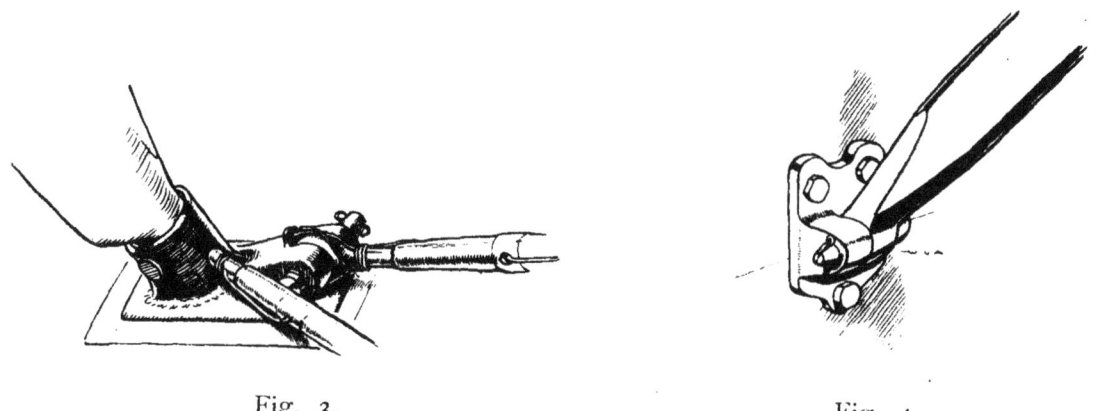

Fig. 3.   Fig. 4.

The centre section struts are streamline section, and consist of flattened steel tubes, welded together so as to form a triangulated construction. These struts are secured to the fuselage in the manner set forth in Fig. 4. At their upper extremities, as shown in Fig. 5 they terminate in ball and socket joints, the box portions of which are carried on the spars of the top plane centre section.

Fig. 5.

With regard to the strut sockets used in other positions, and as illustrated in Fig. 3, these are of a standardised design, except the tubular socket itself, which is adapted to be welded on to the spar plate at different angles according to circumstances.

The main lift wires are taken from the strut sockets of the upper plane to the bottom edge of the fuselage, and are there anchored to stout clips, of the type shown in Fig. 6. These clips are bent round the bottom of the fuselage longeron, and have a horizontal extension carrying a steel strap which passes right across the fuselage, immediately under its wooden transverse member.

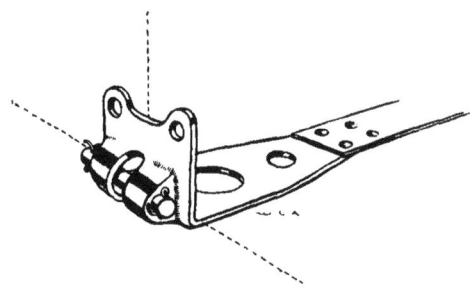

Fig. 6.

FUSELAGE.

This is of approximately rectangular section amidships, tapering off to oval near the tail. It consists of the usual wooden framework of four longerons reinforced and covered in with three-ply wood $\frac{1}{18}$ in. thick. This is applied in square panels in similar manner to that which obtains in the Albatross machines, but in this case is covered all over with doped fabric.

Wiring is absent from this construction, but the fuselage is transversely braced internally with wooden diagonal members, which, however, occur at only one point about half way between the gunner's cockpit and the tail. This is shown in Fig. 7.

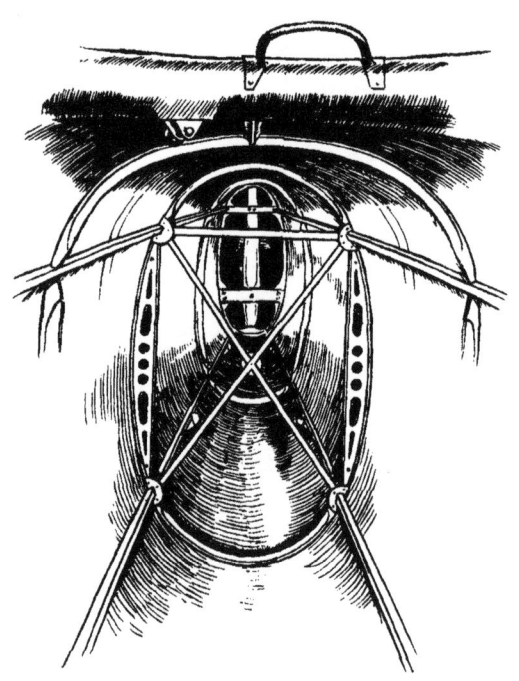

Fig. 7.

At the tail end of the fuselage holes are cut in the covering to facilitate lifting the tail, so that the weight of the machine is carried on the longerons. In Fig. 7 can be seen at the extreme end of the fuselage a strut fastened to cross members. This continues to the top of the fin and forms an attachment for the upper plane of the tail.

The depth of the fuselage at the gunner's cockpit is unusually great, being 4 ft. 7 in., with a width of 3 ft. 2 in. Forward of this point the fuselage is sharply tapered in the vertical plane, but more gently faired off in the horizontal plane.

The engine is only partially covered in.

Between the pilot's and gunner's cockpit is fitted a stout cross member of steel tube.

UNDERCARRIAGE.

This is of the usual design, consisting of tubular steel struts with wooden fairings wrapped on with tape. The forward struts are attached to the fuselage by a joint which also acts as the anchorage of the forward flying wires, and for the undercarriage cross bracing cables. The turnbuckles of the latter are furnished with spherical heads which are carried in ups pressed out of the lug plate. The actual junction of the strut and the socket is formed by a ball and cup.

The shock absorbers are triple coil springs, enclosed in a fabric covering.

The wheels are 760 × 100, and are covered in with fabric discs in the usual manner.

ENGINE MOUNTING.

The engine is carried on I section bearers, bracketted to vertical members of the forward part of the fuselage. One of these bearers is visible through the inspection door, which is shown open in Fig. 5.

ENGINE.

The motor fitted is a 180 H.P. Opel upon which a separate report is issued. It is of standard 6-cylinder vertical type, and is designed on the accepted German lines.

EMPENNAGE.

One of the most characteristic features of the Hannoveraner machine is the biplane tail, of which the span is unusually small. The upper plane is mounted on the fin, which in itself forms a streamline extension of the rearward portion of the fuselage. As in previous German types which have been described, the merging of the stream into the fin is very neatly carried out. The object of the biplane tail is evidently to mitigate the masking effect of the tail on the movable gun, as there is evidence that the gunner habitually fires through the tail at hostile machines approaching from behind. The bottom plane is covered with $\frac{1}{16}$ in. three-ply wood throughout, and the top plane with fabric. The fin is likewise covered with three-ply on which is applied a layer of fabric. Both upper and lower planes are fixed, there being no means of tail adjustment provided.

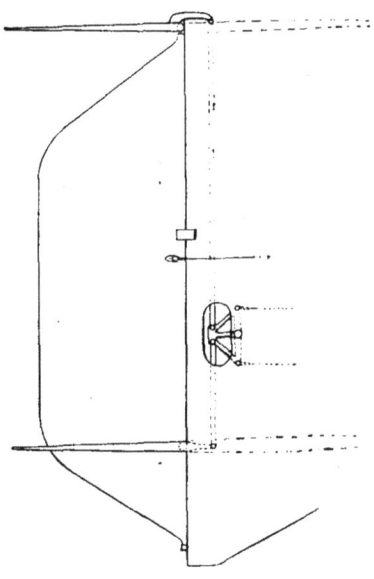

Fig. 8.

Whereas the upper plane is flat and thin, the bottom plane is heavily cambered top and bottom. It is fitted with barbs to prevent mechanics lifting the machine by the tail. An inclined interplane strut is fitted on either side of the fin. This is of steel tube of approximately streamline section, and each cell so formed is furnished with cross bracing wires. That portion of the fin which extends below the fuselage is used to provide the mounting for the tail skid, the general arrangement of the tail being shown in Photograph D. The tail skid is not provided with a swivel mounting, but has a solid metal shoe of good dimensons with convex underside, allowing the skid to sideslip in answer to the rudder when running on the ground. It is sprung with elastic bands at its forward end.

The elevators are worked together, and are coupled up as shown in Fig. 8. It will be noticed that this arrangement, in which the upper and lower links are brought to separate pins, and not to a single pin, results in the elevators being worked through slightly different angles, but this differentiation is in practice, of course, inappreciable.

CONTROL.

The ailerons are fitted to the top plane only. They measure 7 ft. 9½ in. long and project at each side about 7 in. beyond the fixed wing tip. The framework on which they are built consists of light steel tubing. The maximum chord of the aileron is at the wing tip, where it reaches 1 ft. 11 in., having a minimum chord of 1 ft. 6 in. at its inner end. A balancing area of approximately 1 sq. ft. is provided forward of the aileron pivot. The aileron control embodies a curved lever passing through a slot in the main plane immediately ahead of the aileron. From each end of this lever, which forms part of the aileron framework, wires are taken to pulleys on the lower wing, whence they proceed in guides behind the leading wing spar to the control stick, to which they are attached in such a manner that each aileron is actuated positively by a direct pull from the control stick, and not through the medium of a balancing wire.

The control lever is of a type not previously found in German models. As shown in Fig. 9, it is provided with two inclined wooden handles, one of which, on the left side, is not fixed, but is carried by a tubular sleeve which is capable of rotation around the control stick tube. By moving this lever circumferentially, the throttle is controlled by means of a crank which is carried at the bottom end of the control stick sleeve. The throttle lever is fitted with a ratchet operated by a grip lever, as shown in the sketch.

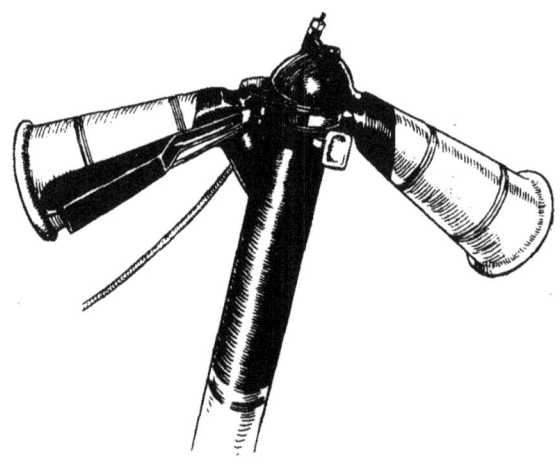

Fig. 9.

The elevators are controlled by the usual double-ended cranks, the wires being carried down the fuselage in small tubular guides.

The rudder bar is built up of welded sheet steel, and is fitted with the usual heel rests. It is placed forward of the bulkhead, which provides a dashboard in front of the pilot's seat, and on each side, as shown in sketch, Fig. 10, sheet metal casings are provided for the pilot's feet. This construction, which is, of course, dictated by considerations of body length, has the advantage of preventing the draught which usually comes from the underside of the pilot's cockpit.

The rudder control wires pass over pulleys on either side of the base of the cockpit, and thence down the fuselage to the rudder.

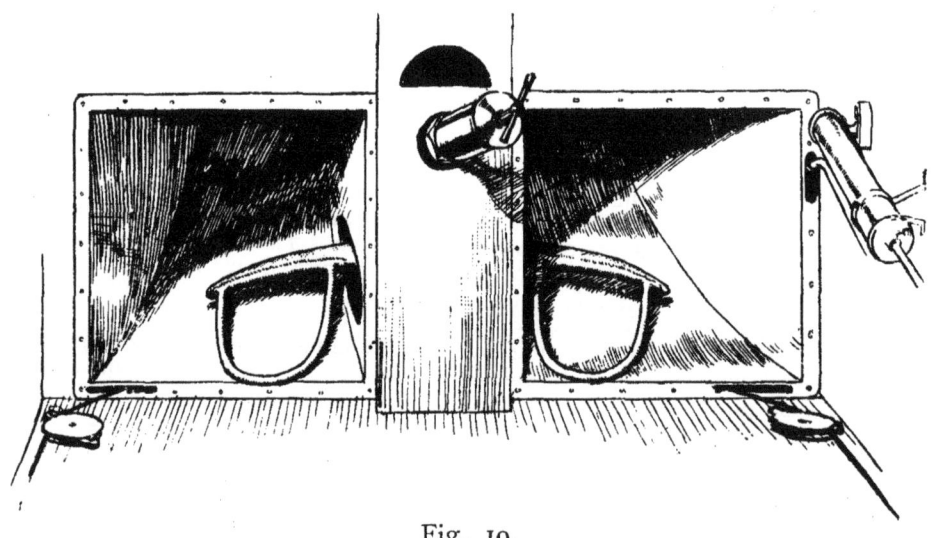

Fig. 10.

ENGINE CONTROL.

The main throttle control is as described above. In addition, however, there is an independent throttle control, consisting of a push rod carried through an opening on the dashboard. Either control can be used independently.

The ignition advance lever is similarly arranged, and consists of a rod thrust through a plate on the dashboard and terminating in a small fibre handle.

RADIATOR.

In accordance with the usual practice characteristic of German machines of this type, the radiator forms a part of the upper plane centre section. It has an area of 27 in by 16 in. by in. deep, and consists of the usual oval section horizontal tubes.

Underneath the radiator and attached to the underside of the centre section is a circular grooved ring. This is evidently intended to carry a semicircular disc which is pivoted in a bearing fixed in the side of the radiator, and the object of which is to act as a controllable radiator shutter.

PETROL SYSTEM.

The main petrol tank has a capacity of 30 gallons, and is fitted under the pilot's seat. It is circular in section. On the left-hand side of the top plane centre section close beside the radiator is a subsidiary tank, feeding by gravity to the carburettor. This is used for starting-up purposes. On its underside it carries a simple form of level indicator.

The main tank feeds the carburettor by air pressure, which is normally .25 grs. per sq. cm.

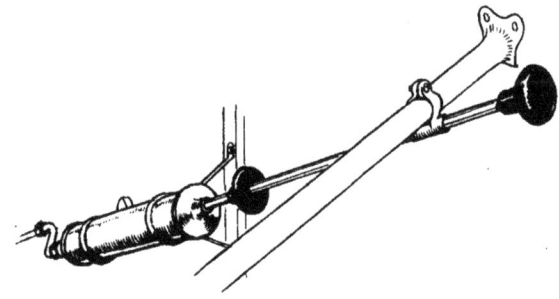

Fig. 11.

A hand air pump is mounted on the right-hand side of the pilot's cockpit, and as shown in sketch, Fig. 11, is fitted with a long handle so as to be worked by either the pilot or the observer.

The main tank is furnished with a Maximall petrol level gauge employing the principle of a float operating a dial by means of a cable passing over pulleys and enclosed in a sealed piping system.

Provision is made for filling the gravity tank from the main tank by means of a semi-rotary hand pump mounted on the left side of the pilot's seat. Taps are arranged so that the carburettors can be fed from either tank.

OIL.

This is contained in a tank on the starboard side of the engine. A glass level gauge is built into the side of the tank, and the covering of the fuselage is cut away at this point so that the oil level is easily visible.

WIRELESS.

No wireless fittings were found in this machine, but it is adapted to take the apparatus when required.

On the rear end of the engine crankshaft is a driving pulley, which can be brought into action by a clutch operated from the observer's seat.

A bracket fitted on the port side of the engine over the rudded bar is evidently intended to carry the dynamo. The latter would also provide surrent for heating, plugs for this purpose being arranged conveniently to both pilot and observer.

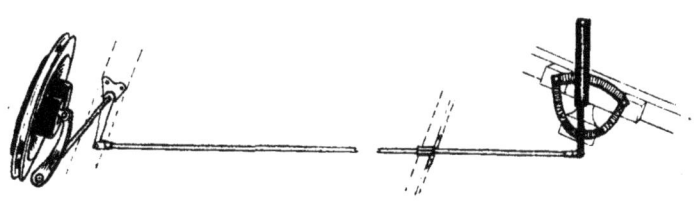

OBSERVER'S COCKPIT.

The observer is provided with a spring-up folding seat, which is so low, that when seated the observer has his head level with the gun mounting. A sketch of this seat is given in Fig. 12.

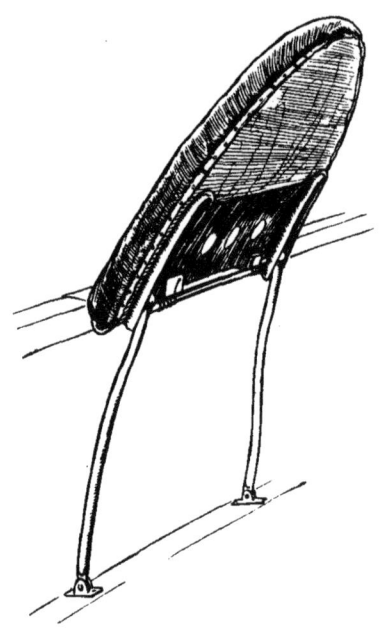

Fig. 12.

Provision is made for the use of a camera through a hole in the bottom of the cockpit. This is normally covered by a sliding panel, which is operated by a return wire running over a pulley. The label shown in Fig. 13 carries the following inscription:—

> "This machine is arranged for photographic utensils (apparatus, implements, etc., not camera) of the Photographic Department. The cross tubes in the observer's cockpit low down in front are easily taken down."

The clips for holding these cross tubes are shown in Fig. 13.

A small board about 12 ins. square can be let down from the back of the pilot's seat for writing purposes, and shuts up out of the way when not required.

Clips are provided for carrying maps, etc.

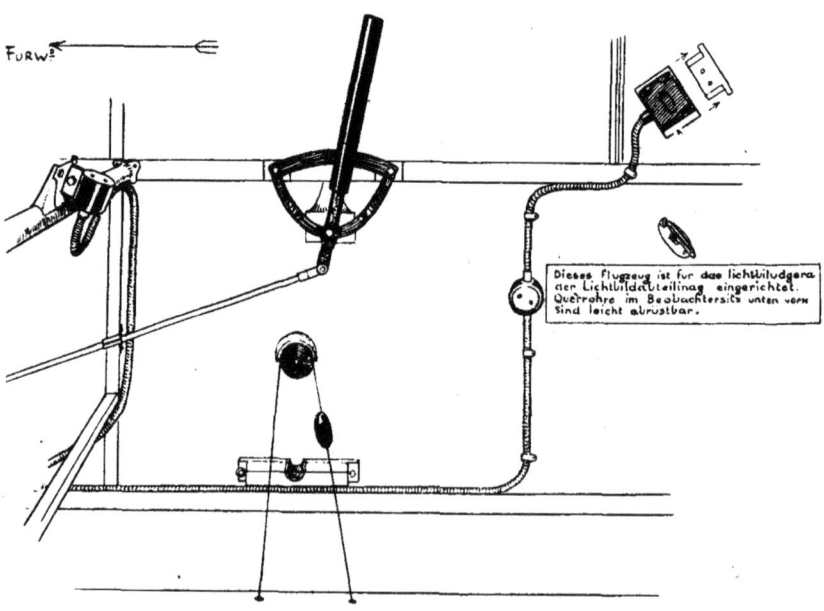

Fig. 13.

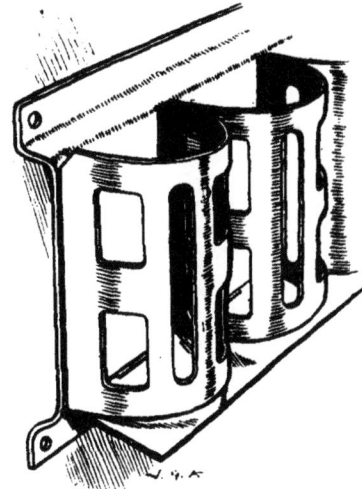

Fig. 14.   Fig. 15.

On the right-hand side of the observer's cockpit is a small pull lever, shown in Fig. 14. In its normal position this rod projects through the side of the fuselage and supports on its outside the hinged bottom of a series of metal pockets, made as shown in Fig. 15. It is not quite clear what purpose is answered by this fitting. Whatever the pockets contain would be simultaneously discharged on pulling the lever.

INSTRUMENTS.

An air speed indicator of the revolving anemometer type, by Morell, of Leipsic, is fitted on the forward left-hand wing strut, where it is readily visible by both the pilot and the observer. The mounting and general design of this instrument is shown in the photograph I.

With this exception, the instruments fitted on the machine, comprising engine revolution counter, compass, barometer, etc., are all of standard type, and have already been reported upon.

PROPELLER.

This is stamped 180 P.S. Argus. It is composed of laminations alternately ash and some species of soft pine.

FABRIC AND DOPE.

Both appear to be of good quality, and are up to the usual German standard.

CAMOUFLAGE.

As will be seen from the photographs, the main planes are camouflaged with the usual mosaic of colours, yellow, green, pink and blue. These colours are dyed into the fabric before doping, and a similar decoration is painted on the fabric of the fuselage, which is generally dark-greenish in colour.

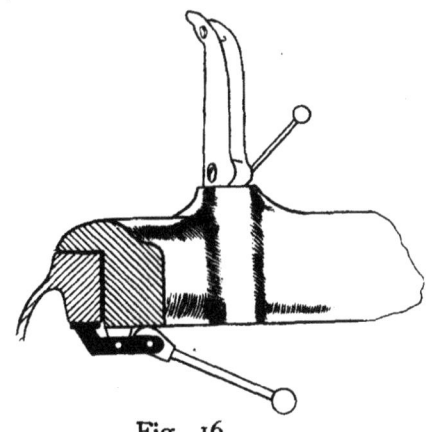

Fig. 16.

ARMAMENT.

The armament consists of a Spandau gun, firing forward through the propeller under the control of the pilot, and a movable gun on a wooden mounting under the control of the observer. The fixed gun is placed close to the exhaust ports of the engine. The mounting of the movable gun is clearly shown in Photograph F, and in Fig. 16.

W. G. A. (Ap.D.L.).
July, 1918.
J. G. WEIR,
Lieut.-Colonel.
Controller, Technical Department.

Photograph A.

Photograph B.

Photograph C.

Photograph D.

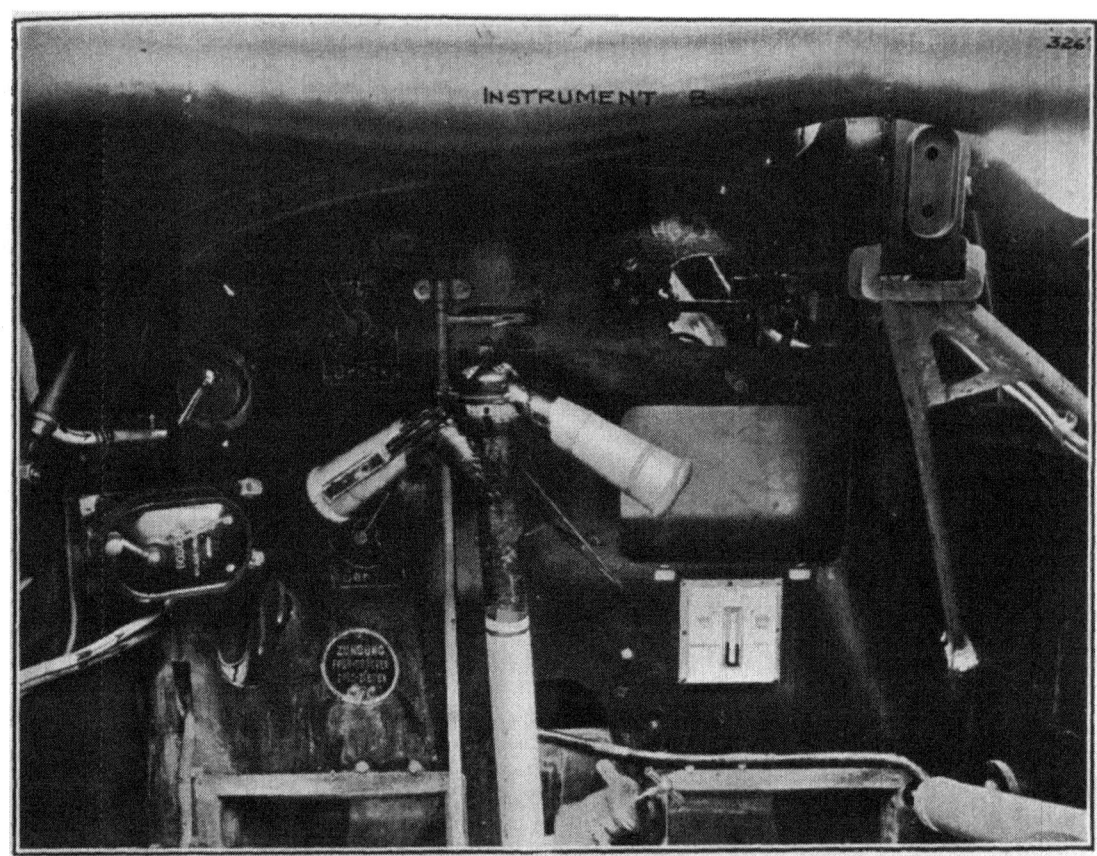

Photograph E.

Photograph F.

Photograph G.

Photograph H.

Photograph I.

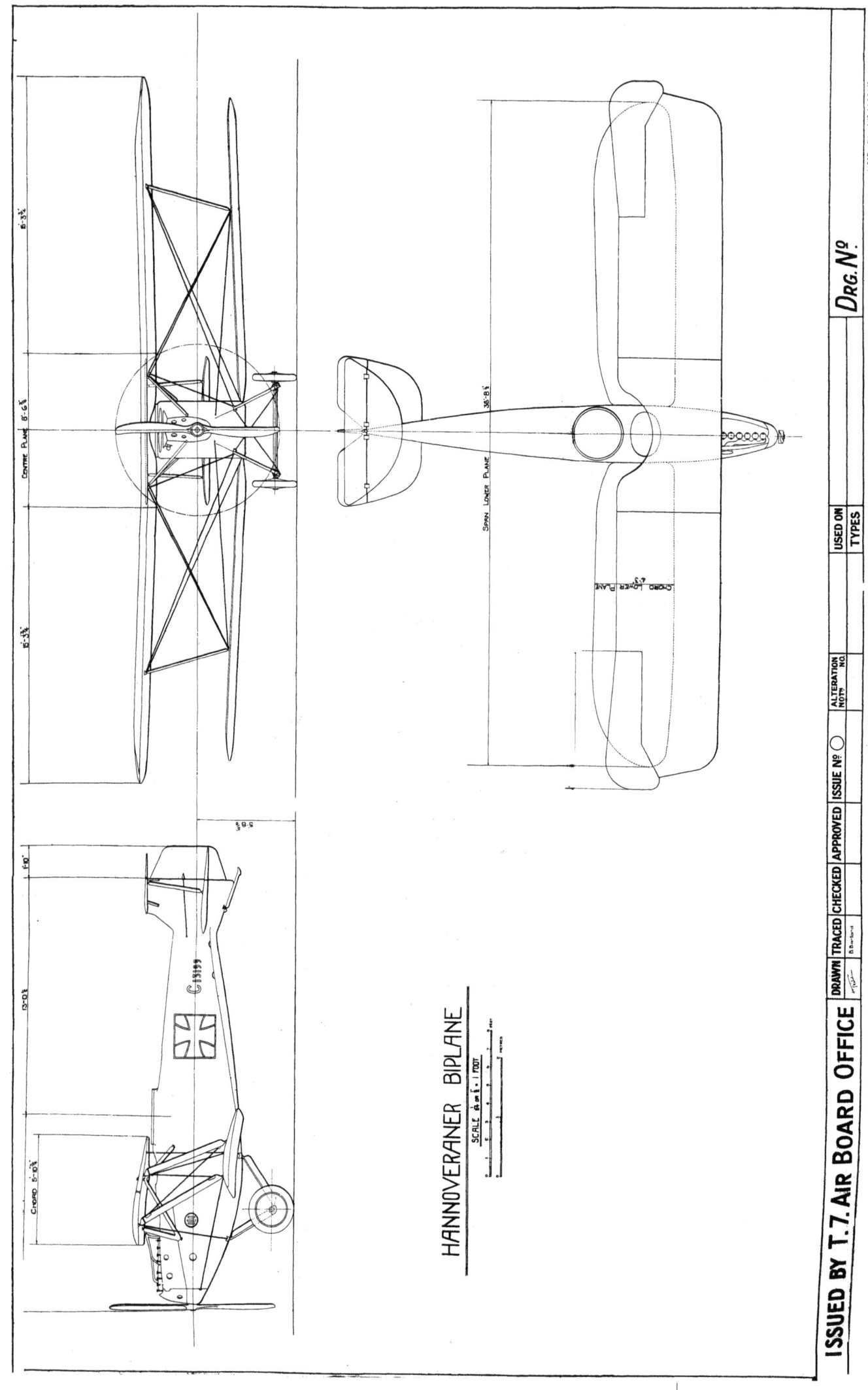

www.ingramcontent.com/pod-product-compliance
Ingram Content Group UK Ltd.
Pitfield, Milton Keynes, MK11 3LW, UK
UKHW051525180426
11947UKWH00019B/1590